Quilts for Kids:
From Crib to College

LEISURE ARTS, INC.
Maumelle, Arkansas

Help children grow up knowing the special warmth that only quilts can provide. This collection includes designs for babies, kids, and college students.

EDITORIAL STAFF
Senior Product Director: Pam Stebbins
Creative Art Director: Katherine Laughlin
Publications Director: Leah Lampirez
Technical Editors: Jean Lewis and Lisa Lancaster
Editorial Writer: Susan Frantz Wiles
Art Category Manager: Lora Puls
Prepress Technician: Stephanie Johnson

BUSINESS STAFF
President and Chief Executive Officer: Fred F. Pruss
Senior Vice President of Operations: Jim Dittrich
Vice President of Retail Sales: Martha Adams
Chief Financial Officer: Tiffany P. Childers
Controller: Teresa Eby
Information Technology Director: Brian Roden
Director of E-Commerce: Mark Hawkins
Manager of E-Commerce: Robert Young

ISBN-13/EAN: 978-1-4647-3535-6

UPC: 0-28906-06479-7

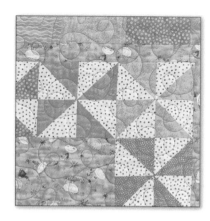

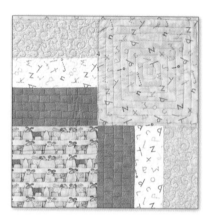

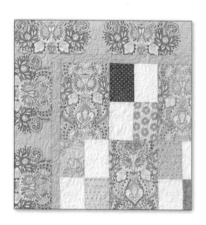

Designed by Me & My Sister Designs, Barbara Groves & Mary Jacobson.

Crazy forBaby

SHOPPING LIST

Yardage is based on 43"/44" (109 cm/112 cm) wide fabric with a usable width of 40" (102 cm).

- ☐ $1^1/_8$ yds (1 m) of orange novelty print fabric
- ☐ $^5/_8$ yd (57 cm) of white polka-dot fabric
- ☐ $^1/_4$ yd (23 cm) each of 6 orange print fabrics
- ☐ $3^3/_8$ yds (3.1 m) of fabric for backing
- ☐ $^1/_2$ yd (46 cm) of fabric for binding
- ☐ 54" x 60" (137 cm x 152 cm) piece of batting

Finished Quilt Size: $45^1/_2$" x $51^1/_2$" (116 cm x 131 cm)
Finished Block Size: 6" x 6" (15 cm x 15 cm)

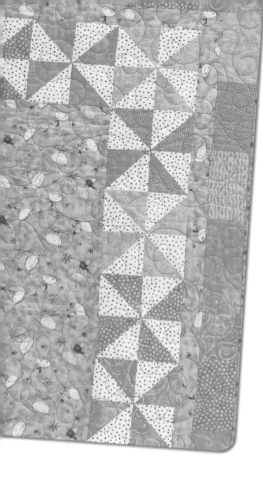

CUTTING OUT THE PIECES

*Follow **Rotary Cutting**, page 51, to cut fabric. Cut all strips from the selvage-to-selvage width of the fabric. All measurements include ¹/₄" seam allowances.*

From orange novelty print fabric:
- Cut 1 **center rectangle** 24¹/₂" x 30¹/₂".
- Cut 5 **border strips** 2"w.

From white polka-dot fabric:
- Cut 5 strips 3⁷/₈"w. From these strips, cut 44 **squares** 3⁷/₈" x 3⁷/₈".

From each of 4 of the 6 orange print fabrics:
- Cut 1 strip 3⁷/₈"w. From this strip, cut 8 **squares** 3⁷/₈" x 3⁷/₈".
- Cut 1 strip 3¹/₂"w. From this strip, cut 6 **rectangles** 3¹/₂" x 5¹/₂".

From each of the 2 remaining orange print fabrics:
- Cut 1 strip 3⁷/₈"w. From this strip, cut 6 **squares** 3⁷/₈" x 3⁷/₈".
- Cut 1 strip 3¹/₂"w. From this strip, cut 6 **rectangles** 3¹/₂" x 5¹/₂".

From fabric for binding:
- Cut 6 **binding strips** 2¹/₄"w.

··

MAKING THE BLOCKS

*Follow **Piecing**, page 52, and **Pressing**, page 53, to make Blocks. Use ¹/₄" seam allowances throughout.*

1. Draw diagonal line (corner to corner) on wrong side of each white polka-dot **square**. With right sides together, place 1 white polka-dot **square** on top of 1 orange print **square**. Stitch seam ¹/₄" from each side of drawn line **(Fig. 1)**.

Fig. 1

2. Cut along drawn line and press seam allowance to darker fabric to make 2 **Triangle-Squares**. Make 88 Triangle-Squares.

Triangle-Squares (make 88)

3. Sew 4 matching **Triangle-Squares** together to make **Block**. Make 22 Blocks.

Block (make 22)

ASSEMBLING THE QUILT TOP CENTER

1. Sew 5 Block's together to make **Unit 1**. Make 2 Unit 1's.

Unit 1 (make 2)

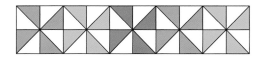

2. Sew 6 Block's together to make **Unit 2**. Make 2 Unit 2's.

Unit 2 (make 2)

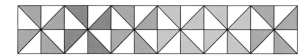

3. Referring to the **Quilt Top Diagram** sew 1 Unit 1 to each side of **center rectangle**, and then sew 1 Unit 2 to top and bottom to complete the **quilt top center**.

ADDING THE BORDERS

1. Sew **border strips** together, end to end, to make 1 continuous **inner border strip**.

2. To determine length of side inner borders, measure length across center of quilt top center. Cut 2 **side inner borders** the determined length from inner border strip. Matching centers and corners, sew side inner borders to quilt top center.

3. To determine length of top/bottom inner borders, measure width across center of quilt top (including added borders). Cut 2 **top/bottom inner borders** the determined length from inner border strip. Matching centers and corners, sew top/bottom inner borders to quilt top center.

4. Sew 9 rectangles together to make **outer border**. Make 4 outer borders.

Outer Border (make 4)

5. Matching centers and corners and easing any fullness, sew side, top, and then bottom outer borders to the quilt top.

COMPLETING THE QUILT

1. Follow **Quilting**, page 54, to mark, layer, and quilt as desired. The model is machine quilted in a loop pattern.

2. If desired, follow **Adding a Hanging Sleeve**, page 58, to add a hanging sleeve.

3. Follow **Binding**, page 58, to make and then attach **straight-grain binding**.

Quilt Top Diagram

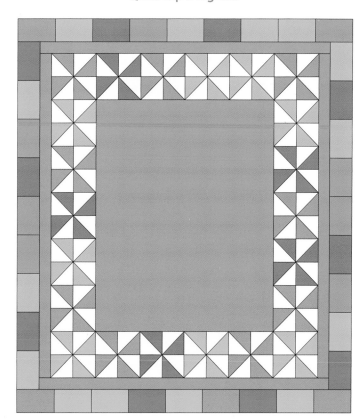

Designed by Me & My Sister Designs,
Barbara Groves & Mary Jacobson.

First
Step

SHOPPING LIST

Yardage is based on 43"/44" (109 cm/112 cm) wide fabric with a usable width of 40" (102 cm).

- ☐ 1 yd (91 cm) of turquoise novelty print fabric
- ☐ ³/₄ yd (69 cm) of turquoise small print fabric
- ☐ ⁵/₈ yd (57 cm) of orange print fabric
- ☐ ⁵/₈ yd (57 cm)) of green print fabric
- ☐ ¹/₂ yd (46 cm) of white print fabric
- ☐ ¹/₂ yd (46 cm) of fabric for binding
- ☐ 3¹/₂ yds (3.2 m) of fabric for backing
- ☐ 62" x 62" (157 cm x 157 cm) square of batting

Finished Size: 54¹/₄" x 54¹/₄" (138 cm x 138 cm)

Turn to page 11 to see this quilt in pastels and pink and green.

CUTTING OUT THE PIECES

*Follow **Rotary Cutting**, page 51, to cut fabric. Cut all strips from the selvage-to-selvage width of the fabric. Wide and narrow strips are cut longer than needed, and will be trimmed after assembling borders. All measurements include 1/4" seam allowances.*

From turquoise novelty print fabric:
- Cut 1 **center square** 32" x 32".

From turquoise small print fabric:
- Cut 2 strips 11 1/2"w. From these strips, cut 4 **corner squares** 11 1/2" x 11 1/2".

From orange print fabric:
- Cut 4 **wide strips** 4 1/2" x 34".

From green print fabric:
- Cut 4 **wide strips** 4 1/2" x 34".

From white print fabric:
- Cut 4 **narrow strips** 3 1/2" x 34".

From fabric for binding:
- Cut 6 **binding strips** 2 1/4"w.

MAKING THE BORDERS

*Follow **Piecing**, page 52, and **Pressing**, page 53, to make borders. Use 1/4" seam allowances throughout.*

1. Sew 1 orange **wide strip**, 1 white **narrow strip**, and 1 green **wide strip** together to make **border**. Trim border to 32". Make 4 borders.

Border
(make 4)

2. Sew 1 **corner square** to each end of 2 borders to make **top/bottom borders**.

Top/Bottom Borders
(make 2)

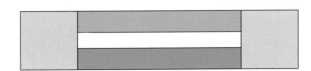

ASSEMBLING THE QUILT TOP

Refer to photo, page 4, to assemble the quilt top.

1. Matching centers and corners, sew remaining borders to **center square**.

2. Matching centers and corners, sew top/bottom borders to center square.

COMPLETING THE QUILT

1. Follow **Quilting**, page 54, to mark, layer, and quilt as desired. The model is machine quilted. Wiggly lines are quilted across the center square, a brick pattern is quilted in the orange strips, meandering quilting alternated with a bubble pattern is quilted in the white strips, and a curlicue pattern is quilted in the green strips. A square spiral is quilted in each corner square.

2. If desired, follow **Adding a Hanging Sleeve**, page 58, to add a hanging sleeve.

3. Follow **Binding**, page 58, to make and then attach **straight-grain binding**.

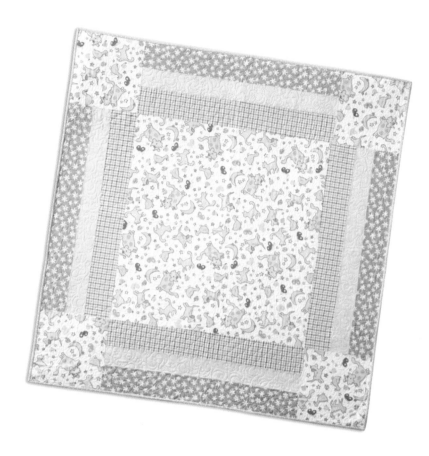

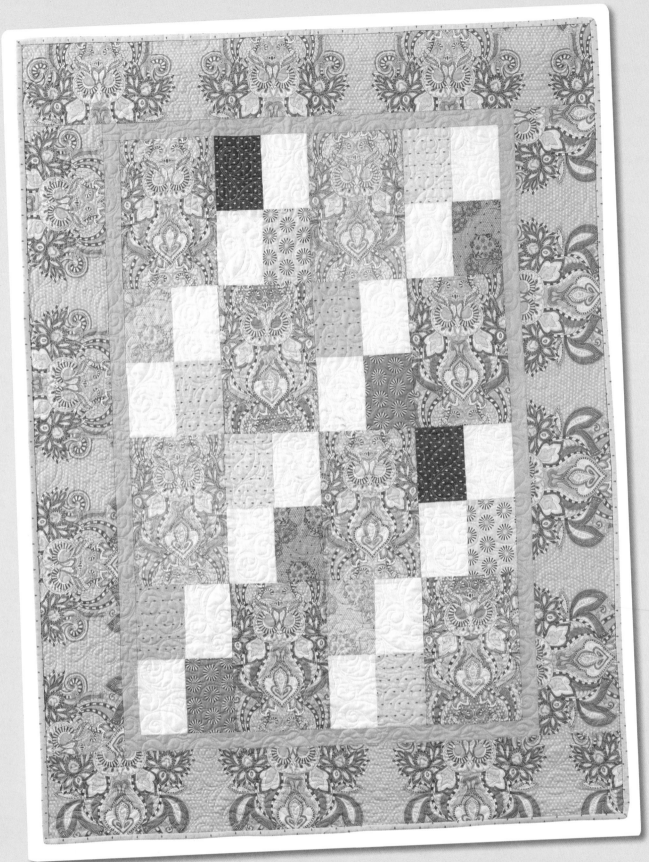

Designed by Ann D. Hansen.

Josie's Quilt
baby size

SHOPPING LIST

Yardage is based on 43"/44" (109 cm/112 cm) wide fabric with a usable width of 40" (102 cm). Fat quarters are approximately 21" x 18" (53 cm x 46 cm).

- ☐ 4 assorted print fat quarters

- ☐ 8 assorted 8" x 6" (20 cm x 15 cm) small print rectangles: 1 brown, 1 pink/brown, **2** pinks, 2 greens, and 2 aquas

- ☐ ¼ yd (23 cm) of white solid fabric

- ☐ ¾ yd (69 m) of green print fabric

- ☐ ¼ yd (23 cm) of pink solid fabric

- ☐ ⅜ yd (34 cm) of pink dot fabric

- ☐ 3¼ yds (3 m) of fabric for backing

- ☐ 45" x 57" (114 cm x 145 cm) piece of batting

Finished Quilt Size: 37" x 49" (94 cm x 124 cm)
Finished Block Size: 6" x 9" (15 cm x 23 cm)

CUTTING

*Follow **Rotary Cutting**, page 51, to cut fabric. Cut all strips from the selvage-to-selvage width of the fabric. All measurements include ¹/₄" seam allowances.*

From each fat quarter:
- Cut 2 **large rectangles** 6¹/₂" x 9¹/₂".

From each small print rectangle:
- Cut 2 **small rectangles** 3¹/₂" x 5".

From white solid fabric:
- Cut 2 strips 3¹/₂" wide. From these strips, cut 16 **small rectangles** 3¹/₂" x 5".

From green print fabric:
- Cut 2 **top/bottom outer borders** 5¹/₂" x 36¹/₂".
- Cut 2 **side outer borders** 5¹/₂" x 38¹/₂".

From pink solid fabric:
- Cut 2 **top/bottom inner borders** 1¹/₂" x 26¹/₂".
- Cut 2 **side inner borders** 1¹/₂" x 36¹/₂".

From pink dot fabric:
- Cut 5 **binding strips** 2¹/₄" wide.

MAKING THE BLOCKS

*Follow **Piecing**, page 52, and **Pressing**, page 53. Use a ¹/₄" seam allowance throughout.*

1. Sew 2 white **small rectangles,** 1 brown **small rectangle** and 1 pink/brown **small rectangle** together to make **Block A**. Make 2 Block A's.

2. Repeat Step 1 using 2 white **small rectangles** and 2 assorted pink **small rectangles** to make **Block B**. Make 2 Block B's.

3. Repeat Step 1 using 2 white **small rectangles** and 2 assorted aqua **small rectangles** to make **Block C**. Make 2 Block C's.

4. Repeat Step 1 using 2 white **small rectangles** and 2 assorted green **small rectangles** to make **Block D**. Make 2 Block D's.

Block A
(make 2)

Block B
(make 2)

Block C
(make 2)

Block D
(make 2)

ASSEMBLING THE QUILT TOP

*Refer to **Quilt Top Diagram** to assemble the quilt top.*

1. Sew 2 **large rectangles,** 1 Block A, and 1 Block B together to make **Row 1**. Make 2 Row 1's.

Row 1 (make 2)

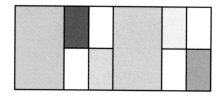

2. Sew 2 **large rectangles,** 1 Block C, and 1 Block D together to make **Row 2**. Make 2 Row 2's.

Row 2 (make 2)

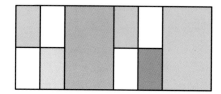

3. Alternating Rows 1 and 2, sew Rows together to make **quilt top center.**

4. Matching centers and corners, sew **side** then **top/bottom inner borders** to quilt top center.

5. Matching centers and corners, sew **side** then **top/bottom outer borders** to quilt top center to complete **quilt top.**

COMPLETING THE QUILT

1. Follow **Quilting**, page 54, to mark, layer, and quilt as desired. The model is machine quilted with an all-over leaf and swirl pattern.

2. If desired, follow **Adding A Hanging Sleeve**, page 58, to add a hanging sleeve.

3. Use **binding strips** and follow **Binding**, page 58, to make and attach **straight-grain binding.**

Quilt Top Diagram

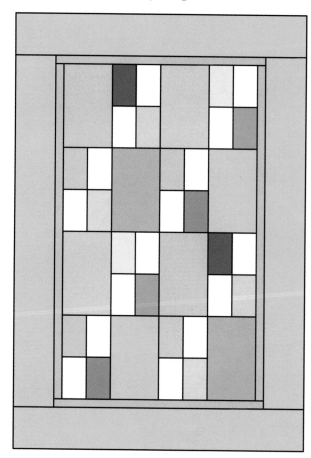

Designed by Ann D. Hansen.

Josie's
Quilt
Child size

SHOPPING LIST

Yardage is based on 43"/44" (109 cm/112 cm) wide fabric with a usable width of 40" (102 cm). Fat quarters are approximately 21" x 18" (53 cm x 46 cm).

- ☐ 6 assorted print fat quarters
- ☐ $5/8$ yd (57 cm) of green dot fabric
- ☐ $1/4$ yd (23 cm) of purple dot fabric
- ☐ $5/8$ yd (57 cm) of uneven stripe fabric
- ☐ $1^3/4$ yds (1.6 m) of wide stripe fabric
- ☐ $4^1/4$ yds (3.9 m) of fabric for backing
- ☐ 57" x 75" (145 cm x 191 cm) piece of batting

Finished Quilt Size: 49" x 67" (124 cm x 170 cm)
Finished Block Size: 6" x 9" (15 cm x 23 cm)

CUTTING

*Follow **Rotary Cutting**, page 51, to cut fabric. Cut all strips from the selvage-to-selvage width of the fabric. All measurements include $1/4$" seam allowances.*

From each fat quarter:
- Cut 3 **rectangles** $6^1/2$" x $9^1/2$".

From green dot fabric:
- Cut 5 **strips** $3^1/2$" wide.

From purple dot fabric:
- Cut 2 **top/bottom inner borders** $1^1/2$" x $36^1/2$".
- Cut 2 **side inner borders** $1^1/2$" x $56^1/2$", piecing as necessary.

From uneven stripe fabric:
- Cut 5 **strips** $3^1/2$" wide.

From wide stripe fabric:
- Cut 2 **top/bottom outer borders** $5^1/2$" x $38^1/2$".
- Cut 2 **side outer borders** $5^1/2$" x $66^1/2$", piecing as necessary.
- Cut 1 **binding square** 24" x 24".

MAKING THE BLOCKS

*Follow **Piecing**, page 52, and **Pressing**, page 53. Use a $1/4$" seam allowance throughout.*

1. Matching long edges, sew 1 green dot **strip** and 1 uneven stripe **strip** together to make **Strip Set**. Make 5 Strip Sets. Cut across Strip Sets at 5" intervals to make **Unit 1**. Make 36 Unit 1's.

   Strip Set
   (make 5)

   Unit 1
   (make 36)

   5"

2. Referring to **Block A Diagram,** sew 2 Unit 1's together to make **Block A**. Make 9 Block A's.

   Block A
   (make 9)

3. Referring to **Block B Diagram,** sew 2 Unit 1's together to make **Block B**. Make 9 Block B's.

   Block B
   (make 9)

ASSEMBLING THE QUILT TOP

*Refer to **Quilt Top Diagram** to assemble the quilt top.*

1. Sew 3 Block A's and 3 **rectangles** together to make **Row 1**. Make 3 Row 1's.

Row 1 (make 3)

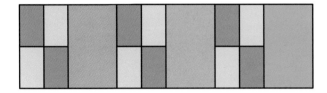

2. Sew 3 Block B's and 3 **rectangles** together to make **Row 2**. Make 3 Row 2's.

Row 2 (make 3)

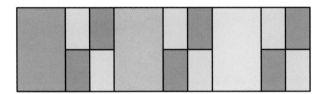

3. Alternating Rows 1 and 2, sew Rows together to make **quilt top center**.

4. Matching centers and corners, sew **top/bottom** then **side inner borders** to quilt top center.

5. Matching centers and corners, sew **top/bottom** then **side outer borders** to quilt top center to complete the **quilt top**.

COMPLETING THE QUILT

1. Follow **Quilting**, page 54, to mark, layer, and quilt as desired. The model is machine quilted with an all-over flower and leaf pattern.

2. If desired, follow **Adding A Hanging Sleeve**, page 58, to add a hanging sleeve.

3. Use **binding square** and follow **Binding**, page 58, to make and attach **bias binding**.

Quilt Top Diagram

Designed by Peggy Waltman,
Hopskotch Quilting Co.

Sixties
Charm

SHOPPING LIST

Yardage is based on 43"/44" (109 cm/112 cm) wide fabric with a usable width of 40" (102 cm).

- [ ] ³/₄ yd (69 cm) of white/blue print (Hourglass Blocks)
- [ ] ³/₄ yd (69 cm) of pink print (Hourglass Blocks)
- [ ] ¹/₂ yd (46 cm) **total** of assorted white/pink prints (Pinwheel Blocks)
- [ ] ¹/₂ yd (46 cm) **total** of assorted pink prints (Pinwheel Blocks)
- [ ] ⁵/₈ yd (57 cm) **total** of assorted blue prints (Pinwheel Blocks)
- [ ] ¹/₄ yd (23 cm) of pink print (Border)
- [ ] ⁵/₈ yd (57 cm) of blue print (Border)
- [ ] 3³/₈ yds (3.1 m) of backing fabric
- [ ] ³/₄ yd (69 cm) of binding fabric
- [ ] 59" x 59" (150 cm x 150 cm) square of batting

Finished Quilt Size: 50¹/₂" x 50¹/₂" (128 cm x 128 cm)
Finished Block Size: 6" x 6" (15 cm x 15 cm)

CUTTING OUT THE PIECES

*Follow **Rotary Cutting**, page 51, to cut fabric. All strips are cut across the width of the fabric. All measurements include $1/4$" seam allowances.*

From white/blue print:
- Cut 3 strips $7^1/4$" wide. From these strips, cut 12 **squares** (**A**) $7^1/4$" x $7^1/4$".

From pink print:
- Cut 3 strips $7^1/4$" wide. From these strips, cut 12 **squares** (**B**) $7^1/4$" x $7^1/4$".

From assorted white/pink prints:
- Cut 25 squares $4^1/4$" x $4^1/4$". Cut each square *twice* diagonally to make 100 **triangles** (**C**).

From assorted pink prints:
- Cut 25 squares $4^1/4$" x $4^1/4$". Cut each square *twice* diagonally to make 100 **triangles** (**D**).

From assorted blue prints:
- Cut 25 sets of 2 matching squares $3^7/8$" x $3^7/8$". Cut each square *once* diagonally to make 100 **triangles** (**E**).

From pink print for border:
- Cut 5 **border strips** (**F**) $1^1/2$" wide.

From blue print for border:
- Cut 5 **border strips** (**G**) $3^1/2$" wide.

From binding fabric:
- Cut 1 **binding square** (**H**) 24" x 24".

MAKING THE HOURGLASS BLOCKS

*Follow **Machine Piecing**, page 52, and **Pressing**, page 53. Use a $1/4$" seam allowance throughout.*

1. Draw a diagonal line in both directions on wrong side of each **square** (**A**). With right sides together, place 1 **square** (**A**) on top of 1 **square** (**B**). Stitch $1/4$" from each side of 1 drawn line (**Fig. 1**).

Fig. 1

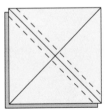

2. Cut apart along drawn line; open and press seam allowances toward white/blue print triangle to make 2 **Triangle-Square A's**. Make 24 **Triangle-Square A's**.

Triangle-Square A (make 24)

 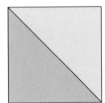

3. On wrong side of 12 **Triangle-Square A's**, extend drawn line from corner of white/blue print triangle to corner of pink print triangle.

4. Match 1 *marked* **Triangle-Square A** and 1 *unmarked* **Triangle-Square A** with white/blue triangles opposite each other and marked Triangle-Square A on top. Stitch ¼" from each side of drawn line (**Fig. 2**). Cut apart along drawn line to make 2 **Hourglass Blocks**. Open and press seam allowances toward one side. Make 24 Hourglass Blocks.

Fig. 2

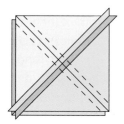

Hourglass Blocks (make 24)

 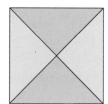

MAKING THE PINWHEEL BLOCKS

1. Sew 1 **triangle (C)** and 1 **triangle (D)** together as shown to make **Unit 1**. Press seam allowances toward triangles (**C**). Make 25 sets of 4 matching **Unit 1's**.

Unit 1 (make 25 sets of 4 matching)

2. Sew 1 **Unit 1** and 1 **triangle (E)** together to make **Unit 2**. Press seam allowances toward larger triangle. Make 25 sets of 4 matching **Unit 2's**.

Unit 2 (make 25 sets of 4 matching)

3. Lay out 4 matching **Unit 2's** to make **Pinwheel Block**. Sew 2 Unit 2's together to make **Unit 3**. Make 2 Unit 3's. Press seam allowances toward blue print triangles. Sew two Unit 3's together to make **Pinwheel Block**. Make 25 **Pinwheel Blocks**. Press seam allowances toward one side.

Unit 3

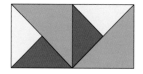

Block (make 25)

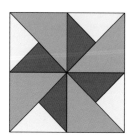

ASSEMBLING THE QUILT TOP CENTER

*Refer to **Quilt Top Diagram**, page 25, for placement.*

1. Beginning with a Pinwheel Block and alternating blocks, sew 4 **Pinwheel Blocks** and 3 **Hourglass Blocks** together to make **Row A**. Press seam allowances toward Hourglass Blocks. Make 4 **Row A's**.

Row A (make 4)

2. Beginning with an Hourglass Block and alternating blocks, sew 4 **Hourglass Blocks** and 3 **Pinwheel Blocks** together to make **Row B**. Press seam allowances toward Hourglass Blocks. Make 3 **Row B's**.

Row B (make 3)

3. Beginning with a Row A and alternating rows, sew 4 **Row A's** and 3 **Row B's** together to make **quilt top center**. Press seam allowances to one side.

ADDING THE BORDERS

1. Sew **border strips (F)** together end to end to make 1 inner border strip.

2. To determine length of inner side borders, measure **length** of quilt top center. From long inner border strip, cut 2 **inner side borders** the determined length. Matching centers and corners, sew inner side borders to quilt top center.

3. To determine length of inner top/bottom borders, measure **width** of quilt top center (including added borders). From remaining long inner border strip, cut 2 **inner top/bottom borders** the determined length. Matching centers and corners, sew inner top/bottom borders to quilt top center.

4. Repeat **Steps 1 – 3** using **border strips (G)** to add outer border.

COMPLETING THE QUILT

1. Follow **Quilting**, page 54, to mark, layer, and quilt as desired. The model was machine quilted with a free-motion design featuring spirals, curves and hearts.

2. If desired, follow **Adding A Hanging Sleeve**, page 58, to add a hanging sleeve.

3. Follow **Binding**, page 58, to make and attach bias binding with mitered corners.

Designed by Tammy Tadd.

Campfire
Blues

SHOPPING LIST

Yardage is based on 43"/44" (109 cm/112 cm) wide fabric with a usable width of 40" (102 cm).

- ☐ $3\frac{1}{8}$ yards (2.9 m) dark-blue print (includes binding)
- ☐ 1 yard (91 cm) red print
- ☐ 2 yards (1.8 m) light-blue print
- ☐ $1\frac{1}{2}$ yards (1.4 m) gold print
- ☐ $4\frac{5}{8}$ yards (4.2 m) backing fabric
- ☐ Template plastic
- ☐ Fine-point permanent marker
- ☐ Fabric marking pencil
- ☐ 64" x 82" (163 cm x 208 cm) batting

Finished quilt size: 56" x 74" (142 cm x 188 cm)
Finished block size: 8" (20 cm)

CUTTING OUT THE PIECES

*Follow **Rotary Cutting**, page 51, to cut fabrics. Follow **Template Cutting**, page 51, to use templates patterns, pages 32-35. Measurements include $1/4$" seam allowances. Cut lengths for borders are exact. You may wish to allow an extra 2" in length for "insurance," and then trim the borders to fit when you add them to the quilt center.*

From dark blue print fabric:

- Cut 2 strips $4^7/8$" wide. Cut these strips to make 12 $4^7/8$" squares. Cut each square in half diagonally to make 24 $4^7/8$" **triangles**.
- Cut 2 **strips** $2^1/4$" wide.
- Cut 2 strips $8^1/2$" wide. Cut these strips into 38 $1^1/2$" x $8^1/2$" **rectangles**.
- Cut 2 strips $2^1/2$" wide, and then trim these strips to make 2 $2^1/2$" x $35^1/2$" **strips**.
- Cut 3 strips $2^1/2$" wide. Piece these strips, and then cut them to make 2 $2^1/2$" x $53^1/2$" **strips**.
- Cut 7 strips $2^1/2$" wide. Piece these strips, and then cut the following strips:
  - 2 $2^1/2$" x $69^1/2$" **strips**
  - 2 $2^1/2$" x $51^1/2$" **strips**
- Cut 2 strips $5^1/2$" wide. From these strips, cut 12 of **template C**.
- Cut 2 strips 4" wide. From these strips, cut 12 of **template F**.
- Cut 7 **binding strips** 2" wide.

From red print fabric:

- Cut 2 strips $4^7/8$" wide. Cut these strips to make 12 $4^7/8$" squares. Cut each square diagonally to make 24 $4^7/8$" **triangles**.
- Cut 2 **strips** $2^1/4$" wide.
- Cut 3 strips $2^1/2$" wide. Cut these strips to make 48 $2^1/2$" **squares**.
- Cut 1 strip $1^1/2$" wide. Cut this strip to make 15 $1^1/2$" **squares**.
- Cut 1 strip $6^1/2$" wide. Cut this strip to make the following squares:
  - 4 $6^1/2$" **squares**
  - 8 $2^1/2$" **squares**

From light blue print fabric:

- Cut 3 strips $3^7/8$" wide. Cut these strips to make 24 $3^7/8$" squares. Cut each square diagonally to make 48 $3^7/8$" **triangles**.
- Cut 2 strips $2^7/8$" wide. Cut these strips to make 24 $2^7/8$" squares. Cut each square diagonally to make 48 $2^7/8$" **triangles**.
- Cut 6 **strips** $1^1/2$" wide.
- Cut 6 strips $6^1/2$" wide. Cut these strips to make the following pieces:
  - 6 of **template A**
  - 6 of **template D**
  - 6 of **template A** reversed*
  - 6 of **template D** reversed*

*When you cut templates A and D reversed, place the template **face up** on **wrong side** of fabric to mark.

From gold print fabric:

- Cut 3 strips $4^7/8$" wide. Cut these strips to make 96 1" x $4^7/8$" **rectangles**.
- Cut 6 **strips** $1^1/2$" wide.
- Cut 6 strips $3^3/4$" wide. From these strips, cut the following pieces:
  - 12 of **template B**
  - 12 of **template E**

MAKING THE BLOCKS

*Follow **Piecing**, page 52, and **Pressing**, page 53, to make the quilt top. Use ¼" seam allowances throughout.*

Block A

1. Sew 1 1" x 4⅞" gold **rectangle** to each short side of a 3⅞" light-blue **triangle** to make **Unit 1**. Make 48.

Unit 1 (make 48)

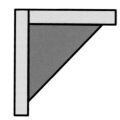

2. With right sides together, place 1 4⅞" red **triangle** on top of 1 Unit 1. Sew a ¼" seam along the long side of the triangles. Trim the gold fabric as needed, and press open the triangle square. Make 24 **red triangle squares**.

Red Triangle Square (make 24)

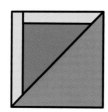

3. Repeat Step 2 using 4⅞" dark-blue **triangles** to make 24 **dark-blue triangle squares**.

4. Referring to the **Block A** diagram, assemble 2 red triangle squares and 2 dark-blue triangle squares to complete **Block A**. Make 12.

Block A (make 12)

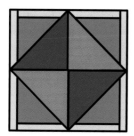

Block B

1. Sew 1 2¼" dark-blue strip and 1 2¼" red strip together to make a **Strip Set**. Make 2 Strip Sets.

Strip Set (make 2)

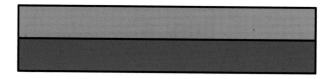

2. Cut these strip sets crosswise at 2¼" intervals to make 24 2¼" x 4" **Unit 2** rectangles.

Unit 2 (make 24)

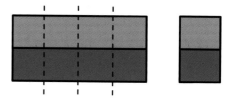

3. Sew 2 Unit 2's together to make a **Four-Patch Unit**. Make 12.

Four-Patch Unit (make 12)

4. Using the square template, page 32, position the template over the Four-Patch Unit so that the cutout area is centered over the intersection of the seams. Align the 4 dotted lines with the 4 seams. Trim the four-patch unit even with the edges of the template **(Fig. 4)**. Repeat for each four-patch unit.

Fig. 4

5. Sew the long side of 1 2⅞" light-blue **triangle** to each side of the Four-Patch Unit to make **Unit 3**. Make 12.

Unit 3 (make 12)

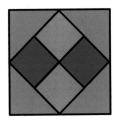

6. Sew 1 1½" light-blue **strip** and 1 1½" gold **strip** together to make a **Strip Set**. Make 6.

7. Cut these strip sets crosswise at 4½" intervals to make 48 2½" x 4½" **Unit 4** rectangles.

8. Sew 1 2½" red **square** to each end of a Unit 4 to make **Unit 5**. Make 24.

Unit 5 (make 24)

9. Sew 1 Unit 4 to each of 2 sides of a Unit 3 to make **Unit 6**. Make 12.

Unit 6 (make 12)

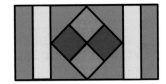

10. Sew 1 Unit 5 to the top and bottom of a Unit 6 to complete **Block B**. Make 12.

Block B (make 12)

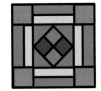

ASSEMBLING THE QUILT CENTER

1. Sew together 2 of **Block A**, 2 of **Block B**, and 3 1½" x 8½" dark-blue rectangles to make a **Row**. Make 6.

Row (make 6)

2. Sew together 4 1½" x 8½" dark-blue rectangles and 3 1½" red squares to make a **sashing strip**. Make 5.

Sashing Strip (make 5)

3. Sew the Rows and the sashing strips together to complete the **quilt top center**. Note that 3 rows are reversed so that Blocks A and B alternate.

Quilt Top Center

ASSEMBLING THE BORDERS
The quilt has 3 borders.

Border 1

1. Sew 1 2½" x 53½" dark-blue **strip** to each long side of the quilt top center.
2. Sew 1 2½" red **square** to each end of a 2 ½" x 35½" dark-blue strip to make the **top border**. Repeat to make the **bottom border**.
3. Sew the top/bottom borders to the top and bottom edges of the quilt top center to complete **border 1**.

Border 2

1. Sew 1 **template B** to 1 **template C**, and then sew 1 **template A** to the long side to complete **border unit 1**. Make 6.

Border Unit 1 (make 6)

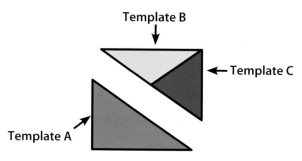

2. Sew 1 template B to 1 template C, and then sew 1 **template A reversed** to the long side to complete **border unit 1 reversed**. Make 6.

Border Unit 1 Reversed (make 6)

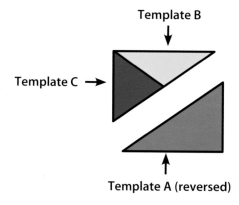

3. Sew 1 **template E** to 1 **template F**, and then sew 1 **template D** to the long side to complete **border unit 2**. Make 6.

Border Unit 2 (make 6)

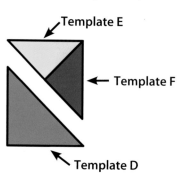

4. Sew 1 template E to 1 template F, and then sew 1 **template D reversed** to the long side to complete **border unit 2 reversed**. Make 6.

Border Unit 2 Reversed (make 6)

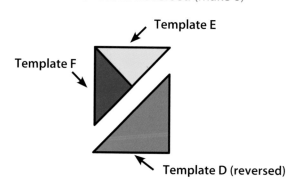

5. Sew 3 border unit 1's and 3 border unit 1's reversed together to make 1 **side border**. Make 2.

Side Border (make 2)

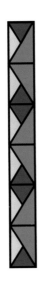

6. Referring to the **Quilt Top Diagram**, page 33, for orientation, sew the side borders to the long sides of the quilt top center.

7. Sew 3 border unit 2's and 3 border unit 2's reversed, and 2 $6^{1}/_{2}$" red squares together to make the **top border**. Repeat to make the **bottom border**.

Top and Bottom Border

8. Sew the top and bottom borders to the top and bottom edges of the quilt top center to complete **border 2**.

Border 3

1. Sew 1 $2^{1}/_{2}$" x $69^{1}/_{2}$" dark-blue-print strip to each long side of the quilt top center.

2. Sew 1 $2^{1}/_{2}$" red square to each end of a $2^{1}/_{2}$" x $51^{1}/_{2}$" dark-blue strip to make the **top border**. Repeat to make the **bottom border**.

3. Sew the top/bottom borders to the top and bottom edges of the quilt top center to complete the **quilt top**.

COMPLETING THE QUILT

1. Follow **Quilting**, page 54, to mark, layer, and quilt as desired. The model was machine quilted with loops and stars in the borders and sashings. There is in-the-ditch quilting in the block centers.

2. Using **binding strips**, follow **Binding**, page 58, to make and then attach **straight-grain binding**.

$3^{3}/_{8}$" Square Template

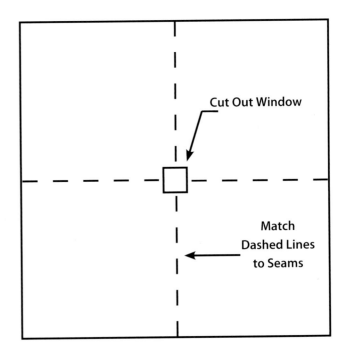

QUILT TOP DIAGRAM

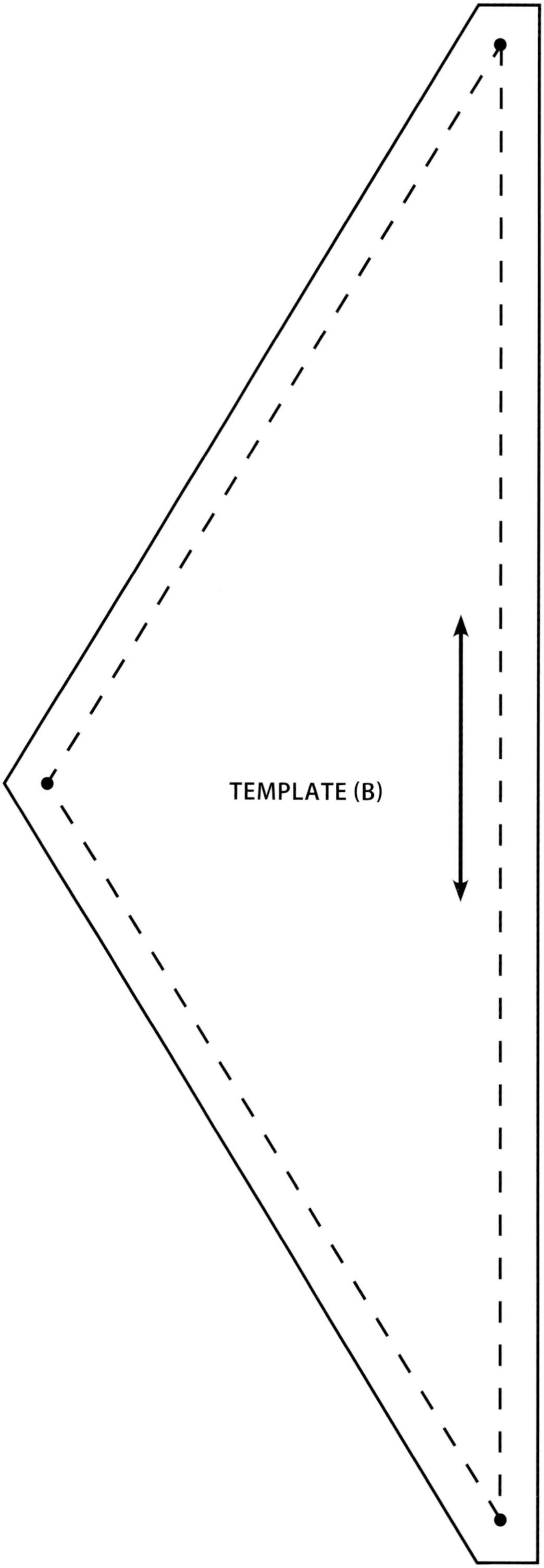

TEMPLATE (B)

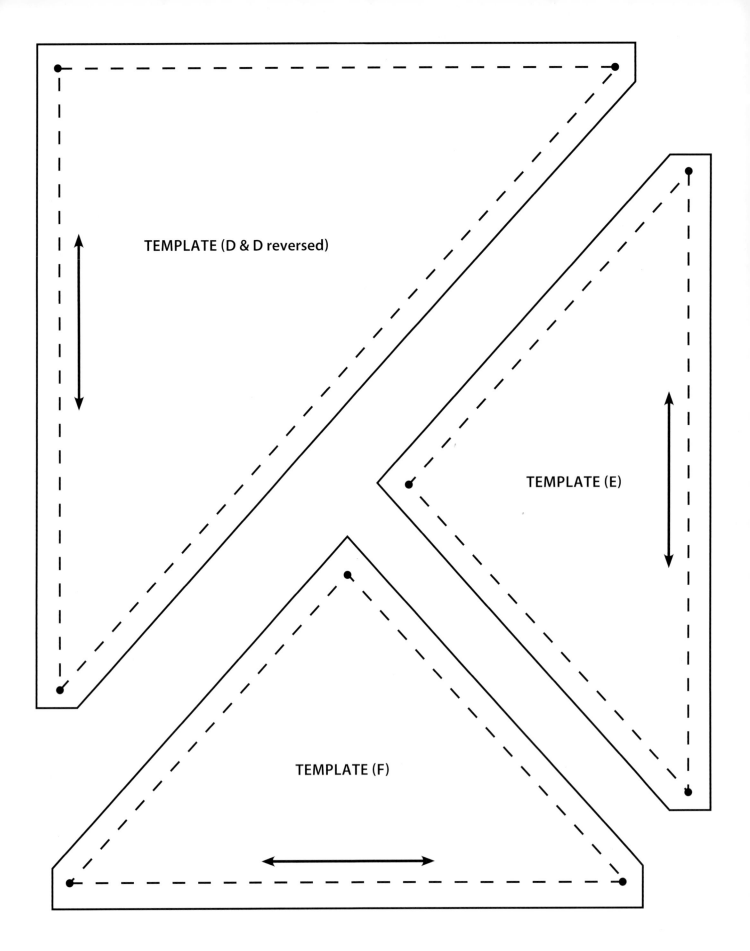

TEMPLATE (D & D reversed)

TEMPLATE (E)

TEMPLATE (F)

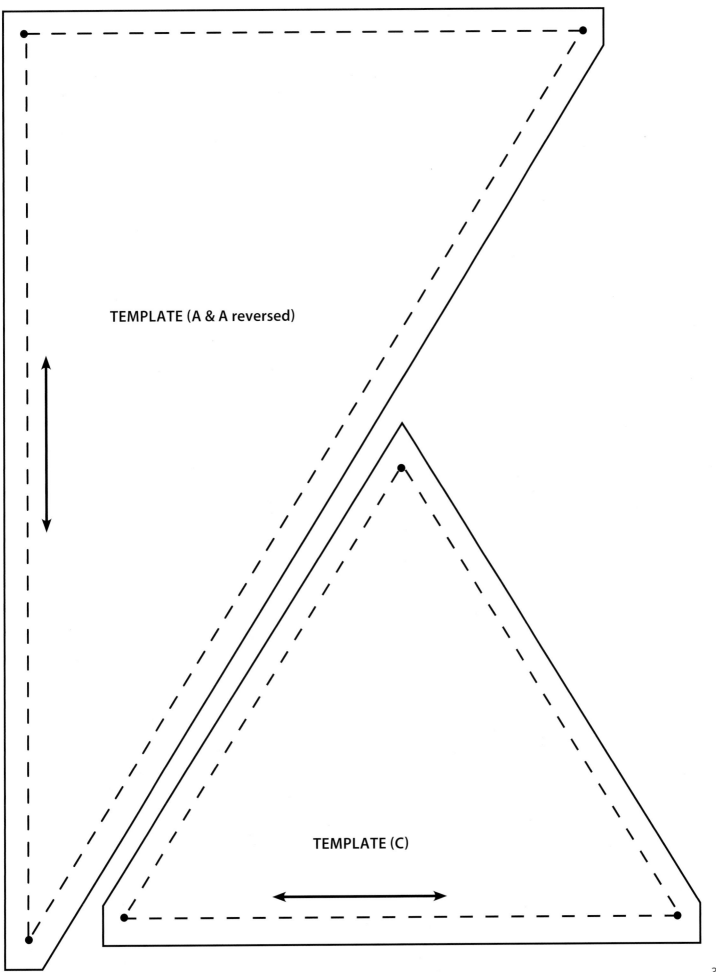

TEMPLATE (A & A reversed)

TEMPLATE (C)

Designed by Tammy Tadd.

Kick theCan

SHOPPING LIST

Yardage is based on 43"/44" (109 cm/112 cm) wide fabric with a usable width of 40" (102 cm).

- ☐ ³/₈ yard (34 cm) each of 7 different multi prints
- ☐ ¹/₂ yard (46 cm) each of 7 different tone-on-tone prints
- ☐ ¹/₂ yard (46 cm) green print
- ☐ 1¹/₄ yards (1.1 m) turquoise print
- ☐ ¹/₂ yard (46 cm) yellow print for binding
- ☐ 4⁵/₈ yards (4.1 m) fabric for backing
- ☐ 62" x 82" (157 cm x 208 cm) piece of batting

Finished quilt size: 54" x 74" (137 cm x 188 cm)
Finished block size: 6" x 8" (15 cm x 20 cm)

CUTTING YOUR FABRICS

*Follow **Rotary Cutting**, page 51, to cut fabrics. Measurements include ¼" seam allowances. Cut lengths for borders are exact. You may wish to allow an extra 2" in length for "insurance," and then trim the borders to fit when you add them to the quilt center.*

From each multi-print fabric:
- Cut 2 strips 4½"w. From these strips, cut 6 **rectangles** 4½" x 8½".

From each tone-on-tone print fabric:
- Cut 2 strips 6"w. From these strips, cut 6 **rectangles** 6" x 8½".
- Cut 1 strip 3½"w. From this strip, cut 6 **rectangles** 3½" x 6".

From each green print fabric
- 2 **strips** 3" x 41½", piecing as needed.
- 2 **strips** 3" x 56½", piecing as needed.

From turquoise print fabric:
- Cut 2 **strips** 6½" x 53½", piecing as needed.
- Cut 2 **strips** 6½" x 61½", piecing as needed.

From yellow print fabric:
- Cut 7 **binding strips** 2"w.

MAKING THE BLOCKS

*Photocopy the foundation patterns for Blocks A and B, pages 42-43. You will need 21 copies of each. You may want to make a few extra copies of each pattern for practice. Refer to **Paper Foundation Piecing**, page xx, to make the paper-pieced blocks.*

Block A

1. For each **Block A**, select 1 multi-print rectangle, 1 6" x 8½" tone-on-tone print rectangle, and 1 3½" x 6" rectangle of the same tone-on-tone print.

2. With the right side facing up, cut each tone-on-tone rectangle in half diagonally (**Fig. 1**).

Fig. 1

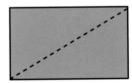

3. Place the wrong side of 1 multi-print rectangle (piece 1) against the unmarked side of the foundation paper for Block A, ensuring that the fabric completely covers the area marked 1 (**Fig. 2**). Pin the fabric in place from the marked side of the foundation paper.

Fig. 2

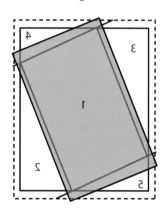

4. Matching right sides of fabric pieces, place a larger tone-on-tone triangle on top of piece 1 (**Fig. 3**). Make sure the fabric extends beyond the outer edges of area 2. Turn over the foundation paper, and pin piece 2 in place from the marked side of the paper.

Fig. 3

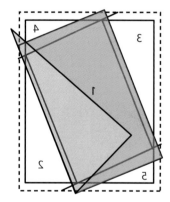

5. With the marked side of the foundation paper face up, sew along the line between areas 1 and 2, extending sewing a few stitches beyond the beginning and end of the line. Open piece 2 and press (**Fig. 4**).

Fig. 4

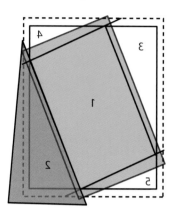

6. Add pieces 3, 4, and 5 in the same manner usingthe remaining large triangle and the 2 smaller triangles. Trim the seam allowances to $1/4$" after you add each piece.

7. Trim the fabric along the dotted lines on the foundation paper to make a $6^1/2$" x $8^1/2$" unfinished **Block A**.

8. Repeat steps 1 through 7 to make a total of 21 **Block A's**.

Block A (make 21)

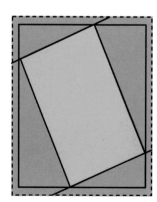

Block B

1. For each **Block B**, select 1 multi-print rectangle, 1 6" x 8$\frac{1}{2}$" tone-on-tone print rectangle, and 1 3$\frac{1}{2}$" x 6" rectangle of the same tone-on-tone print.

2. With the right side facing up, cut each tone-on-tone rectangle in half diagonally in the opposite direction of **Fig. 1**, page 38.

3. Use the foundation papers for **Block B** to make 21 **Block B's**.

Block B (make 21)

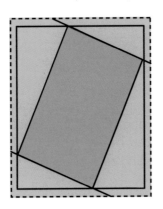

ASSEMBLING THE QUILT TOP CENTER

The quilt has 7 rows of 6 blocks each.

1. Beginning with a **Block A** and alternating the blocks, sew 3 **Block A's** and 3 **Block B's** together, to make **Row 1**. Make 4 Row 1's.

2. Beginning with a **Block B** and alternating the blocks, sew 3 **Block A's** and 3 **Block B's** together, to make **Row 2**. Make 3 Row 2's.

3. Referring to the **Quilt Top Center Diagram** sew the Rows together to complete the **quilt top center**.

4. Carefully remove the foundation paper from the blocks. Tweezers can help you remove paper from the areas where seams intersect.

Quilt Top Center

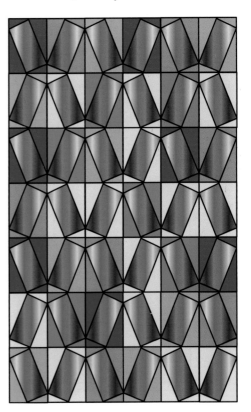

ASSEMBLING THE BORDERS

1. Sew 1 3" x 56¹/₂" green-print strip to each long side of the quilt top center.

2. Sew the 3" x 41¹/₂" green-print strips to the top and bottom of the quilt top center to complete the **inner border**.

3. Sew 1 6¹/₂" x 61¹/₂" turquoise-print strip to each long side of the quilt top center.

4. Sew the 6¹/₂" x 53¹/₂" turquoise-print strips to the top and bottom of the quilt top center to complete the **outer border**.

COMPLETING THE QUILT

1. Follow **Quilting**, page 54, to mark, layer, and quilt as desired. The model has a free-motion graphic design in the outer border, outline quilting in the inner border, and in-the-ditch quilting in the Blocks.

2. **If** desired, follow **Adding a Hanging Sleeve**, page 58, to add a hanging sleeve.

3. Using **binding strips**, follow **Binding**, page 58, to make and then attach **straight-grain binding**.

Quilt Top Diagram

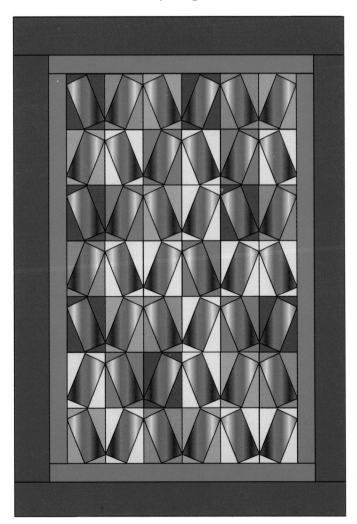

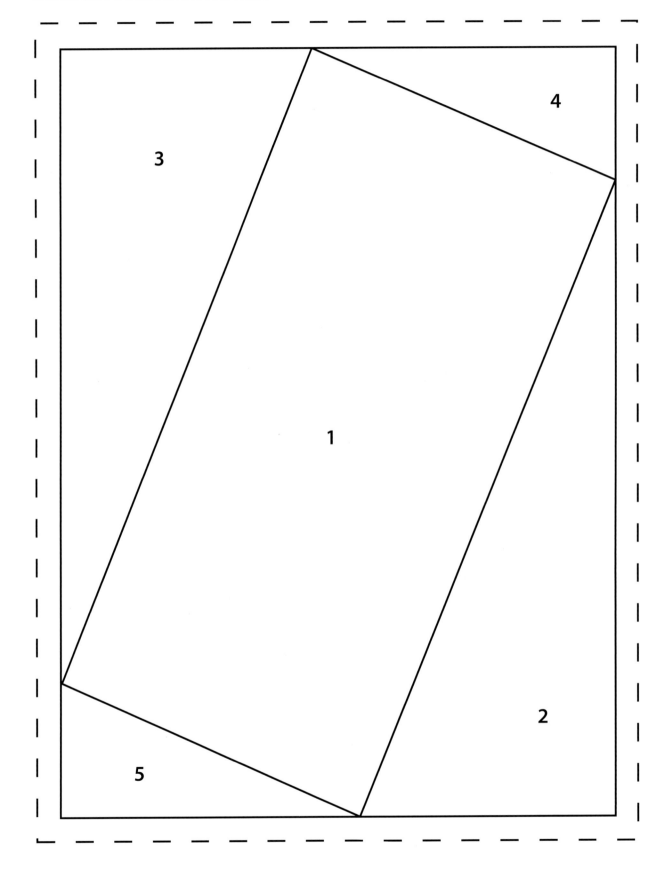

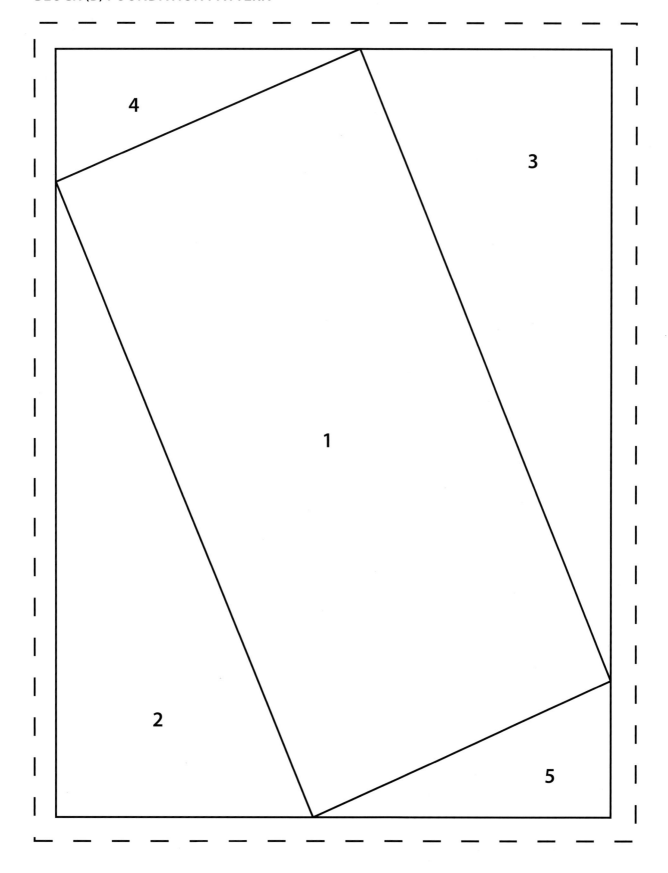

Designed by Gudrun Erla.

Simply
Rectangles
Traditional Version

SHOPPING LIST

Yardage is based on 43"/44" (109 cm/112 cm) wide fabric with a "usable" width of 40" (102 cm). Fat quarters are approximately 21" x 18" (53 cm x 46 cm).

- ☐ $^3/_8$ yard (34 cm) each of 7 different multi prints
- ☐ 15 fat quarters of assorted prints
- ☐ $1^1/_4$ yds (1.1 m) of cream print
- ☐ $4^1/_2$ yds (4.1 m) of fabric for backing
- ☐ $^5/_8$ yd (57 cm) of fabric for binding*
- ☐ 69" x 79" (175 cm x 201 cm) piece of batting

*Straight-grain binding for quilt shown was cut from a diagonally striped fabric.

Finished Lap Quilt Size: 61" x 71" (155 cm x 180 cm)
Finished Block Size: 10" x 14" (25 cm x 36 cm)

CUTTING THE PIECES

*Follow **Rotary Cutting**, page 51. Cut strips from yardage from the selvage-to-selvage width of the fabric. Cut strips from fat quarters parallel to long edge. Measurements include $1/4$" seam allowances.*

From *each* fat quarter:

- Cut 1 strip $4^1/2$" wide. From this strip, cut 2 **center rectangles** $4^1/2$" x $8^1/2$".
- Cut 1 strip $10^1/2$" wide. From this strip, cut 8 **outer rectangles** $2^1/2$" x $10^1/2$".

From cream print:

- Cut 25 strips $1^1/2$" wide. From these strips, cut 60 **large inner rectangles** $1^1/2$" x $8^1/2$" and 60 **small inner rectangles** $1^1/2$" x $6^1/2$".

From fabric for binding:

- Cut 8 **binding strips** $2^1/2$" wide.

MAKING THE BLOCKS

*Follow **Piecing**, page 52, and **Pressing**, page 53, to make the quilt top. Use $1/4$" seam allowances throughout.*

1. For Block, select 4 **outer rectangles** from one print, 1 **center rectangle** from a contrasting print, 2 **large inner rectangles**, and 2 **small inner rectangles**.

2. Sew 2 **large inner rectangles** and 1 **center rectangle** together to make **Unit 1**.

Unit 1

3. Sew 2 **small inner rectangles** and Unit 1 together to make **Unit 2**.

Unit 2

4. Sew 2 **outer rectangles** and Unit 2 together to make **Unit 3**.

Unit 3

5. Sew 2 outer rectangles and Unit 3 together to make **Block**.

6. Repeat Steps 1-5 to make a total of 30 Blocks.

Block (make 30)

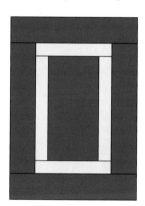

ASSEMBLING THE QUILT TOP
*Refer to **Quilt Top Diagram** to assemble quilt top.*
1. Sew 6 Blocks together to make **Row**. Make 5 Rows.

2. Sew Rows together to complete the **quilt top**.

COMPLETING THE QUILT
1. Follow **Machine Quilting**, page 54, to mark, layer, and quilt as desired. The model was machine quilted with an all-over flower and leaf pattern.

2. If desired, follow **Adding a Hanging Sleeve**, page 58, to add a hanging sleeve.

3. Use **binding strips** and follow **Binding**, page 58, to make and attach **straight-grain binding**.

Quilt Top Diagram

Designed by Gudrun Erla.

Simply
Rectangles
Modern Version

Finished Lap Quilt Size: 61" x 71" (155 cm x 180 cm)
Finished Block Size: 10" x 14" (25 cm x 36 cm)

The modern version of Simply Rectangles is constructed the same as the traditional version, page 44, with the following exceptions.

1. A total of 21 black and white print fat quarters, some with pink, lime green, or red, were used.
2. An accent fabric was not used. Instead, each block contains a center rectangle from one print, inner rectangles from a second print, and outer rectangles from a third print.

General Instructions

To make your quilting easier and more enjoyable, we encourage you to carefully read all of the general instructions, study the color photographs, and familiarize yourself with the individual project instructions before beginning a project.

FABRICS

SELECTING FABRICS

Choose high-quality, medium-weight 100% cotton fabrics. All-cotton fabrics hold a crease better, fray less, and are easier to quilt than cotton/polyester blends.

Yardage requirements listed for each project are based on 43"/44" wide fabric with a "usable" width of 40" after shrinkage and trimming selvages. Actual usable width will probably vary slightly from fabric to fabric. Our recommended yardage lengths should be adequate for occasional re-squaring of fabric when many cuts are required.

PREPARING FABRICS

Prewashing may cause edges to ravel. As a result, your pre-cut fabric pieces may not be large enough to cut all the pieces required for your chosen project. Therefore, we do not recommend pre-washing your yardage or pre-cut fabrics.

Before cutting, prepare fabrics with a steam iron set on cotton and starch or sizing. The starch or sizing will give the fabric a crisp finish. This will make cutting more accurate and may make piecing easier.

ROTARY CUTTING

- Place the fabric on a work surface with the fold closest to you.

- Cut all strips from the selvage-to-selvage width of the fabric unless otherwise indicated in the project instructions.

- Square the left edge of the fabric using a rotary cutter and rulers *(Figs. 1-2)*.

Fig. 1

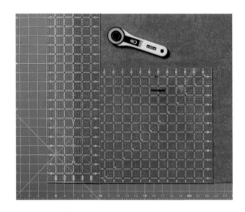

Fig. 2

- To cut each strip required for a project, place the ruler over the cut edge of the fabric, aligning the desired marking on the ruler with the cut edge; make the cut *(Fig. 3)*.

Fig. 3

- When cutting several strips from a single piece of fabric, it is important to make sure that the cuts remain at a perfect right angle to the fold; square the fabric as needed.

TEMPLATE CUTTING

- To make a template from a pattern, lay template plastic over the pattern and trace the pattern with a fine-point permanent marker. Be sure to include all pattern markings. Cut out template along the inner edge of the solid outer line. Repeat to make a template for each pattern in the project instructions.

- To use a template, place the template face up on the wrong side of the fabric. Draw around the template with a removable fabric marking pen or pencil. Repeat for the number of pieces called for in the project instructions.

PIECING

Precise cutting, followed by accurate piecing, will ensure that all pieces of the quilt top fit together well.

MACHINE PIECING

- Set the sewing machine stitch length for approximately 11 stitches per inch.

- Use neutral-colored general-purpose sewing thread (not quilting thread) in the needle and in the bobbin.

- An accurate $1/4$" seam allowance is *essential*. Presser feet that are $1/4$" wide are available for most sewing machines.

- When piecing, always place the pieces right sides together and match the raw edges; pin if necessary.

- Chain piecing saves time and will usually result in more accurate piecing.

- Trim away the points of seam allowances that extend beyond the edges of the sewn pieces.

SEWING STRIP SETS

When there are several strips to assemble into a strip set, first sew the strips together into pairs, then sew the pairs together to form a strip set. To help avoid distortion, sew the seams in opposite directions *(Fig. 4)*.

Fig. 4

SEWING ACROSS SEAM INTERSECTIONS

When sewing across the intersection of two seams, place the pieces right sides together and match seams exactly, making sure seam allowances are pressed in opposite directions *(Fig. 5)*.

Fig. 5

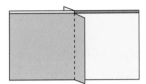

SEWING SHARP POINTS

To ensure sharp points when joining triangular or diagonal pieces, stitch across the center of the "X" (shown in pink) formed on wrong side by previous seams *(Fig. 6)*.

Fig. 6

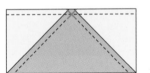

PAPER FOUNDATION PIECING

1. Using the Foundation Pattern(s) for your project, trace or photocopy the pattern(s) the number of times indicated in your project instructions. You can use any lighweight type paper.

2. Use a fine to medium needle (70/80) with a sharp point in your machine and a stitch length of 12-18 stitches per inch.

3. Fabric pieces are always positioned on the unmarked side of the foundation paper for sewing. All stitching will be done on the printed side of the foundation paper, sewing directly on the printed lines.

4. Starting with the lowest number on the foundation paper, position the wrong side of the fabric piece on the unmarked side of the paper by holding the paper towards you (Holding the paper up to a bright light will enable you to see where to place the fabric). Make sure the fabric piece extends at least $1/4$" on all sides of the area the fabric is to cover. Pin the fabric piece to the foundation paper if needed.

5. With the printed side of the foundation paper towards you, place the next fabric piece right side down on the first piece. Again, make sure the fabric is large enough to cover the area and extends at least $1/4$" on all sides.

6. Begin stitching 2 or 3 stitches before and after the sewing line. You do not need to backstitch.

7. Lay the piece on a cutting mat with foundation paper on top. Fold the foundation paper back and trim the the fabric to a scant $1/4$" seam allowance.

8. Finger press the fabric piece you just added over the space it is to cover. Continue to add fabric in numerical order to complete the design.

9. Press the completed piece and trim the edges, leaving a $1/4$" seam allowance beyond the outer solid line.

PRESSING

- Use a steam iron set on "Cotton" for all pressing.

- Press after sewing each seam.

- Seam allowances are almost always pressed to one side, usually toward the darker fabric. However, to reduce bulk it may occasionally be necessary to press the seam allowances toward the lighter fabric or even to press them open.

- To prevent a dark fabric seam allowance from showing through a light fabric, trim the darker seam allowance slightly narrower than the lighter seam allowance.

- To press long seams, such as those in long strip sets, without curving or other distortion, lay the strips across the width of the ironing board.

- When sewing blocks into rows, seam allowances may be pressed in one direction in odd numbered rows and in the opposite direction in even numbered rows. When sewing rows together, press the seam allowances in one direction.

QUILTING

*Quilting holds the three layers (top, batting, and backing) of the quilt together and can be done by hand or machine. Because marking, layering, and quilting are interrelated and may be done in different orders depending on the circumstances, please read the entire **Quilting** section, pages 54-57, before beginning the project.*

TYPES OF QUILTING DESIGNS

In the Ditch Quilting

Quilting along the seamlines or along the edges of appliquéd pieces is called "in the ditch" quilting. This type of quilting should be done on the side *opposite* the seam allowance and does not have to be marked.

Outline Quilting

Quilting a consistent distance, usually $1/4$", from the seam or appliqué is called "outline" quilting. Outline quilting may be marked, or $1/4$" masking tape may be placed along the seamlines for quilting guide. (Do not leave the tape on the quilt longer than necessary, since it may leave an adhesive residue.)

Motif Quilting

Quilting a design, such as a feathered wreath, is called "motif" quilting. This type of quilting should be marked before basting the quilt layers together.

Echo Quilting

Quilting that follows the outline of an appliquéd or pieced design with two or more parallel lines is called "echo" quilting. This type of quilting does not need to be marked.

Channel Quilting

Quilting with straight, parallel lines is called "channel" quilting. This type of quilting may be marked or stitched using a guide.

Crosshatch Quilting

Quilting straight lines in a grid pattern is called "crosshatch" quilting. Lines may be stitched parallel to the edges of quilt or stitched diagonally. This type of quilting may be marked or stitched using a guide.

Meandering Quilting

Quilting in random curved lines and swirls is called "meandering" quilting. Quilting lines should not cross or touch each other. This type of quilting does not need to be marked.

Stipple Quilting

Meandering quilting that is very closely spaced is called "stipple" quilting. Stippling will flatten the area quilted and is often stitched in the background areas to raise the appliquéd or pieced designs. This type of quilting does not need to be marked.

MARKING QUILTING LINES

Quilting lines may be marked using fabric marking pencils, chalk markers, or water- or air-soluble pens.

Simple quilting designs may be marked with chalk or chalk pencil after basting. A small area may be marked, then quilted, before moving to the next area to be marked. Intricate designs should be marked before basting using a more durable marker.

Caution: Pressing may permanently set some marks. **Test** different markers **on scrap fabric** to find one that marks clearly and can be thoroughly removed.

A wide variety of pre-cut quilting stencils, as well as entire books of quilting patterns, are available. Using a stencil makes it easier to mark intricate or repetitive designs.

To make a stencil from a pattern, center template plastic over the pattern and use a permanent marker to trace the pattern onto the plastic. Use a craft knife with a single or double blade to cut channels along the traced lines *(Fig. 7)*.

Fig. 7

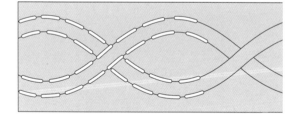

PREPARING THE BACKING

To allow for slight shifting of the quilt top during quilting, the backing should be approximately 4" larger on all sides. Yardage requirements listed for quilt backings are calculated for 43"/44"w fabric. Using 90"w or 108"w fabric for the backing of a bed-sized quilt may eliminate piecing. To piece a backing using 43"/44"w fabric, use the following instructions.

1. Measure the length and width of the quilt top; add 8" to each measurement.

2. If the determined width is 79" or less, cut the backing fabric into two lengths slightly longer than the determined *length* measurement. Trim the selvages. Place the lengths with right sides facing and sew the long edges together, forming a tube *(Fig. 8)*. Match the seams and press along one fold *(Fig. 9)*. Cut along the pressed fold to form a single piece *(Fig. 10)*.

Fig. 8

Fig. 9

Fig. 10

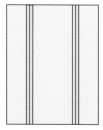

3. If the determined width is more than 79", it may require less fabric yardage if the backing is pieced horizontally. Divide the determined *length* measurement by 40" to determine how many widths will be needed. Cut the required number of widths the determined *width* measurement. Trim the selvages. Sew the long edges together to form a single piece.

4. Trim the backing to the size determined in Step 1; press the seam allowances open.

CHOOSING THE BATTING

The appropriate batting will make quilting easier. For fine hand quilting, choose low-loft batting. All cotton or cotton/polyester blend battings work well for machine quilting because the cotton helps "grip" quilt layers. If the quilt is to be tied, a high-loft batting, sometimes called extra-loft or fat batting, may be used to make the quilt "fluffy."

Types of batting include cotton, polyester, wool, cotton/polyester blend, cotton/wool blend, and silk.

When selecting batting, refer to the package labels for characteristics and care instructions. Cut the batting the same size as the prepared backing.

ASSEMBLING THE QUILT

1. Examine the wrong side of the quilt top closely; trim any seam allowances and clip any threads that may show through the front of the quilt. Press the quilt top, being careful not to "set" any marked quilting lines.

2. Place the backing *wrong* side up on a flat surface. Use masking tape to tape the edges of the backing to the surface. Place the batting on top of the backing fabric. Smooth the batting gently, being careful not to stretch or tear. Center the quilt top *right* side up on the batting.

3. If hand quilting, begin in the center and work toward the outer edges to hand baste all the layers together. Use long stitches and place basting lines approximately 4" apart *(Fig. 11)*. Smooth fullness or wrinkles toward the outer edges.

Fig. 11

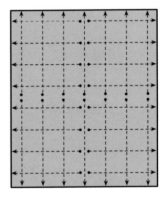

4. If machine quilting, use 1" rustproof safety pins to "pin-baste" all layers together, spacing the pins approximately 4" apart. Begin at the center and work toward outer edges to secure all the layers. If possible, place pins away from the areas that will be quilted, although the pins may be removed as needed when quilting.

MACHINE QUILTING METHODS

Use general-purpose thread in the bobbin. Do not use quilting thread. Thread the needle of machine with general-purpose thread or transparent monofilament thread to make the quilting blend with the quilt top fabrics. Use decorative thread, such as a metallic or contrasting-color general-purpose thread, to make the quilting lines stand out more.

Straight-Line Quilting

The term "straight-line" is somewhat deceptive, since curves (especially gentle ones) as well as straight lines can be stitched with this technique.

1. Set the stitch length for six to ten stitches per inch and attach a walking foot to the sewing machine.

2. Determine which section of the quilt will have the longest continuous quilting line, oftentimes the area from the center top to the center bottom. Roll up and secure each edge of the quilt to help reduce the bulk, keeping the fabrics smooth. Smaller projects may not need to be rolled.

3. Begin stitching on the longest quilting line, using very short stitches for the first $1/4$" to "lock" quilting. Stitch across the project, using one hand on each side of the walking foot to slightly spread the fabric and to guide the fabric through the machine. Lock the stitches at end of the quilting line.

4. Continue machine quilting, stitching longer quilting lines first to stabilize quilt before moving on to other areas.

Free-Motion Quilting

Free-motion quilting may be free form or may follow a marked pattern.

1. Attach a darning foot to the sewing machine and lower or cover the feed dogs.

2. Position the quilt under the darning foot; lower the foot. Holding the top thread, take a stitch and pull the bobbin thread to top of quilt. To "lock" the beginning of the quilting line, hold the top and bobbin threads while making three to five stitches in place.

3. Use one hand on each side of the darning foot to slightly spread the fabric and to move the fabric through the machine. Even stitch length is achieved by using smooth, flowing hand motion and steady machine speed. Slow machine speed and fast hand movement will create long stitches. Fast machine speed and slow hand movement will create short stitches. Move the quilt sideways, back and forth, in a circular motion, or in a random motion to create the desired designs; do not rotate the quilt. Lock stitches at the end of each quilting line.

ADDING A HANGING SLEEVE

Attaching a hanging sleeve to the back of a wall hanging or quilt before the binding is added allows the project to be displayed on a wall.

1. Measure the width of the quilt top edge and subtract 1". Cut a piece of fabric 7"w by the determined measurement.

2. Press the short edges of the fabric piece $1/4$" to the wrong side; press the edges $1/4$" to the wrong side again and machine stitch in place.

3. Matching the wrong sides, fold the piece in half lengthwise to form a tube.

4. Follow the project instructions to sew the binding to the quilt top and to trim the backing and batting. Before Blindstitching the binding to the backing, match the raw edges and stitch the hanging sleeve to the center top edge on the quilt back.

5. Finish binding the quilt, treating the hanging sleeve as part of the backing.

6. Blindstitch the hanging sleeve bottom to the backing, taking care not to stitch through to the quilt front.

BINDING

Binding encloses the raw edges of a quilt. Because of its stretchiness, bias binding works well for binding projects with curves or rounded corners and tends to lie smooth and flat in any given circumstance. Binding may also be cut from the straight lengthwise or crosswise fabric grain.

MAKING BIAS BINDING

Bias strips for binding can simply be cut and pieced to the desired length. However, when a long length of binding is needed, the "continuous" method is quick and accurate.

1. Cut the **binding square** in half diagonally to make two triangles.

2. With the right sides together and using a $1/4$" seam allowance, sew the triangles together *(Fig. 12)*; press the seam allowances open.

Fig. 12

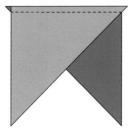

3. On the wrong side of fabric, draw lines the width of the binding as specified in the project instructions, usually $2^1/2$" *(Fig. 13)*. Cut off any remaining fabric less than this width.

Fig. 13

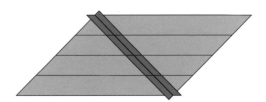

4. With the right sides inside, bring the short edges together to form a tube; match the raw edges so that the first drawn line of the top section meets the second drawn line of the bottom section *(Fig. 14)*.

Fig. 14

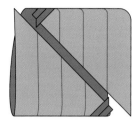

5. Carefully pin the edges together by inserting pins through the drawn lines at the point where the drawn lines intersect, making sure the pins go through the intersections on both sides. Using a $1/4$" seam allowance, sew the edges together; press the seam allowances open.

6. To cut a continuous strip, begin cutting along the first drawn line *(Fig. 15)*. Continue cutting along the drawn line around the tube.

Fig. 15

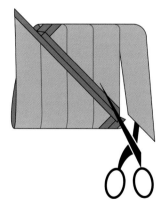

7. Trim the ends of the bias strip square.

8. Matching the wrong sides and raw edges, carefully press the bias strip in half lengthwise to complete the binding.

MAKING STRAIGHT-GRAIN BINDING

1. To piece binding strips, use the diagonal seams method *(Fig. 16)*.

Fig. 16

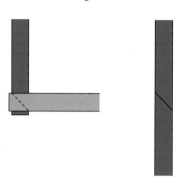

2. Matching the wrong sides and raw edges, press the strip(s) in half lengthwise to complete the binding.

ATTACHING BINDING WITH MITERED CORNERS

1. Beginning with one end near the center on the bottom edge of the quilt, lay the binding around the quilt to make sure that the seams in the binding will not end up at a corner. Adjust placement if necessary. Matching the raw edges of the binding to the raw edge of the quilt top, pin the binding to the right side of the quilt along one edge.

2. When you reach the first corner, mark $1/4$" from the corner of the quilt top *(Fig. 17)*.

Fig. 17

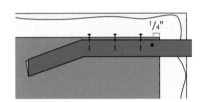

3. Beginning approximately 10" from the end of the binding and using a $1/4$" seam allowance, sew the binding to the quilt, backstitching at the beginning of stitching and at the mark *(Fig. 18)*. Lift the needle out of the fabric and clip the thread.

Fig. 18

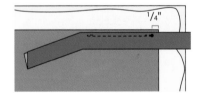

4. Fold the binding as shown in **Figs. 19-20** and pin the binding to the adjacent side, matching the raw edges. When you've reached the next corner, mark $1/4$" from the edge of the quilt top.

Fig. 19

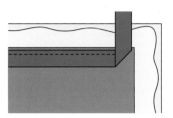

Fig. 20

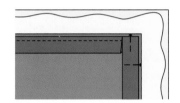

5. Backstitching at the edge of quilt top, sew the pinned binding to the quilt *(Fig. 21)*; backstitch at the next mark. Lift the needle out of the fabric and clip the thread.

Fig. 21

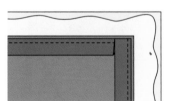

6. Continue sewing the binding to the quilt, stopping approximately 10" from the starting point *(Fig. 22)*.

Fig. 22

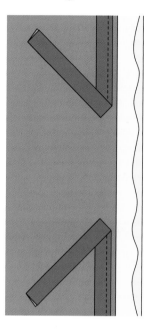

7. Bring the beginning and end of the binding to the center of the opening and fold each end back, leaving a ¼" space between the folds *(Fig. 23)*. Finger press the folds.

Fig. 23

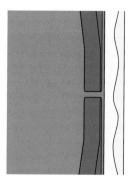

8. Unfold the ends of the binding and draw a line across the wrong side in the finger-pressed crease. Draw a line through the lengthwise pressed fold of binding at the same spot to create a cross mark. With the edge of the ruler at the cross mark, line up the 45° angle marking on the ruler with one long side of the binding. Draw a diagonal line from edge to edge. Repeat on the remaining end, making sure that the two diagonal lines are angled the same way *(Fig. 24)*.

Fig. 24

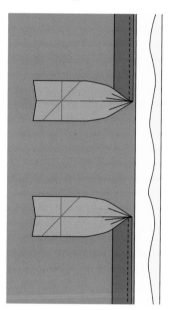

9. Matching the right sides and diagonal lines, pin the binding ends together at right angles *(Fig. 25)*.

Fig. 25

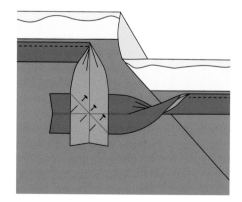

10. Machine stitch along the diagonal line *(Fig. 26)*, removing the pins as you stitch.

Fig. 26

11. Lay the binding against the quilt to double check that it is the correct length.

12. Trim the binding ends, leaving a ¼" seam allowance; press the seam allowances open. Stitch the binding to the quilt.

13. Trim the backing and batting a scant ¼" larger than the quilt top so that the batting and backing will fill the binding when it is folded over to the quilt backing. If using narrower binding, trim the backing and batting even with the quilt top edges.

14. On one edge of the quilt, fold the binding over to the quilt backing and pin the pressed edge in place, covering the stitching line *(Fig. 27)*. On the adjacent side, fold the binding over, forming a mitered corner *(Fig. 28)*. Repeat to pin the remainder of the binding in place.

Fig. 27

Fig. 28

15. Blindstitch the binding to the backing, taking care not to stitch through to the quilt front *(Fig. 29)*.

Fig. 29

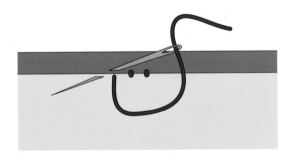

Signing and Dating Your Quilt

A completed quilt is a work of art and should be signed and dated. The label should reflect the style of the quilt, the occasion or person for which it was made, and the quilter's own particular talents. Following are suggestions for recording the history of the quilt or adding a sentiment for future generations.

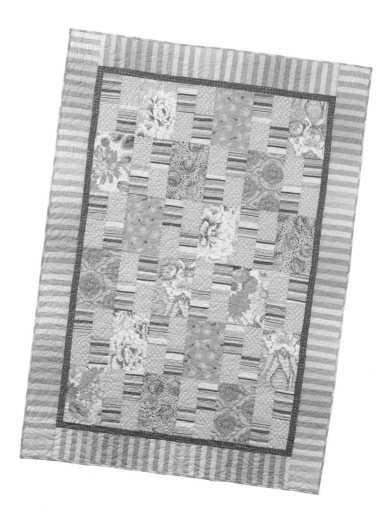

- Embroider the quilter's name, date, and any additional information on the quilt top or backing. Matching floss, such as cream floss on a white border, will leave a subtle record. Bright or contrasting floss will make the information stand out.

- Make a label from muslin and use permanent marker to write the information. Use different colored permanent markers to make the label more decorative. Stitch the label to the quilt back.

- Use photo-transfer paper to add an image to a white or cream fabric label. Stitch the label to the quilt back.

- Piece an extra block from the quilt top pattern to use as a label. Add the information with a permanent fabric pen. Appliqué the block to the quilt back.

- Write a message on an appliquéd design from the quilt top. Attach the appliqué to the quilt back.

Metric Conversion Chart

Inches x 2.54 = centimeters (cm)	Yards x .9144 = meters (m)
Inches x 25.4 = millimeters (mm)	Yards x 91.44 = centimeters (cm)
Inches x .0254 = meters (m)	Centimeters x .3937 = inches (")
	Meters x 1.0936 = yards (yd)

Standard Equivalents

1/8"	3.2 mm	0.32 cm	1/8 yard	11.43 cm	0.11 m
1/4"	6.35 mm	0.635 cm	1/4 yard	22.86 cm	0.23 m
3/8"	9.5 mm	0.95 cm	3/8 yard	34.29 cm	0.34 m
1/2"	12.7 mm	1.27 cm	1/2 yard	45.72 cm	0.46 m
5/8"	15.9 mm	1.59 cm	5/8 yard	57.15 cm	0.57 m
3/4"	19.1 mm	1.91 cm	3/4 yard	68.58 cm	0.69 m
7/8"	22.2 mm	2.22 cm	7/8 yard	80 cm	0.8 m
1"	25.4 mm	2.54 cm	1 yard	91.44 cm	0.91 m